THE 30-MINUTE SHAKESPEARE
THE MERCHANT OF VENICE

"Nick Newlin's work as a teaching artist for Folger Education during the past thirteen years has provided students, regardless of their experience with Shakespeare or being on stage, a unique opportunity to tread the boards at the Folger Theatre. Working with students to edit Shakespeare's plays for performance at the annual Folger Shakespeare Festivals has enabled students to gain new insights into the Bard's plays, build their skills of comprehension and critical reading, and just plain have fun working collaboratively with their peers.

Folger Education promotes performance-based teaching of Shakespeare's plays, providing students with an interactive approach to Shakespeare's plays in which they participate in a close reading of the text through intellectual, physical, and vocal engagement. Newlin's *The 30-Minute Shakespeare* series is an invaluable resource for teachers of Shakespeare, and for all who are interested in performing the plays."

ROBERT YOUNG, PH.D.
DIRECTOR OF EDUCATION
FOLGER SHAKESPEARE LIBRARY

Merchant of Venice: The 30-Minute Shakespeare
ISBN 978-1-935550-32-7
Adaptation, essays, and notes ©2018 by Nick Newlin

Cover design by Sarah Juckniess
Printed in the United States of America

Distributed by Consortium Book Sales & Distribution
www.cbsd.com

NICOLO WHIMSEY PRESS
www.30MinuteShakespeare.com

Art Director: Sarah Juckniess
Managing Editors: Katherine Little, Leah Gordon

THE MOST EXCELLENT HISTORIE
of the

MERCHANT OF VENICE

THE 30-MINUTE SHAKESPEARE

Written by **WILLIAM SHAKESPEARE**

Abridged AND Edited
by **NICK NEWLIN**

Nicolo Whimsey Press
Brandywine, MD

To my grandfather
William G. Foulke
("Grandaddy")

A true gentleman

Special thanks to Joanne Flynn, Bill Newlin, Eliza Newlin Carney, William and Louisa Newlin, Michael Tolaydo, Hilary Kacser, Sarah Juckniess, Katherine Little, Eva Zimmerman, Leah Gordon, Tanya Tolchin, Frank Harris, Julie Schaper and all of Consortium, Leo Bowman and the students, faculty, and staff at Banneker Academic High School, Charlie Feeser, and Robert Young Ph.D. and the Folger Shakespeare Library, especially the wonderful Education Department.

✳ TABLE OF CONTENTS

✳ NO EXPERIENCE NECESSARY

I was not a big "actor type" in high school, so if you weren't either, or if the young people you work with are not, then this book is for you. Whether or not you work with "actor types," you can use this book to stage a lively and captivating thirty-minute version of a Shakespeare play. No experience is necessary.

When I was about eleven years old, my parents took me to see Shakespeare's *Two Gentlemen of Verona*, which was being performed as a Broadway musical. I didn't comprehend every word I heard, but I was enthralled with the language, the characters, and the story, and I understood enough of it to follow along. From then on, I associated Shakespeare with *fun*.

Of course Shakespeare is fun. The Elizabethan audiences knew it, which is one reason he was so popular. It didn't matter that some of the language eluded them. The characters were passionate and vibrant, and their conflicts were compelling. Young people study Shakespeare in high school, but more often than not they read his work like a text book and then get quizzed on academic elements of the play, such as plot, theme, and vocabulary. These are all very interesting, but not nearly as interesting as standing up and performing a scene! It is through performance that the play comes alive and all its "academic" elements are revealed. There is nothing more satisfying to a student or teacher than the feeling of "owning" a Shakespeare play, and that can only come from performing it.

But Shakespeare's plays are often two or more hours long, making the performance of an entire play almost out of the question. One can perform a single scene, which is certainly a good start, but what about the story? What about the changes a character goes through as the play progresses? When school groups perform one scene unedited, or when they lump several plays together, the audience can get lost. This is why I have always preferred to tell the story of the play.

The 30-Minute Shakespeare gives students and teachers a chance to get up on their feet and act out a Shakespeare play in half an hour, using his language. The emphasis is on key scenes, with narrative bridges between scenes to keep the audience caught up on the action. The stage directions are built into this script so that young actors do not have to stand in one place; they can move and tell the story with their actions as well as their words. And it can all be done in a classroom during class time!

That is where this book was born: not in a research library, a graduate school lecture, a professional stage, or even an after-school drama club. All of the play cuttings in *The 30-Minute Shakespeare* were first rehearsed in a D.C. public high school English class, and performed successfully at the Folger Shakespeare Library's annual Secondary School Shakespeare Festival. The players were not necessarily "actor types." For many of them, this was their first performance in a play.

Something almost miraculous happens when students perform Shakespeare. They "get" it. By occupying the characters and speaking the words out loud, students gain a level of understanding and appreciation that is unachievable by simply reading the text. That is the magic of a performance-based method of learning Shakespeare, and this book makes the formerly daunting task of staging a Shakespeare play possible for anybody.

With *The 30-Minute Shakespeare* book series I hope to help teachers and students produce a Shakespeare play in a short amount of time, thus jump-starting the process of discovering the beauty, magic, and fun of the Bard. Plot, theme, and language reveal themselves through the performance of these half-hour play cuttings, and everybody involved receives the priceless gift of "owning" a piece of Shakespeare. The result is an experience that is fun and engaging, and one that we can all carry with us as we play out our own lives on the stages of the world.

NICK NEWLIN
Brandywine, MD
March 2010

CHARACTERS IN THE PLAY

The following is a list of characters that appear in this cutting of *The Merchant of Venice*.

Seventeen actors appeared in the original production. The number can be increased to about thirty or decreased to about twelve by having actors share or double roles.

For the full breakdown of characters, see Sample Program.

LANCELET: Servant to Shylock, and later to Bassanio

ANTONIO: A merchant of Venice

SOLARINO: Companion of Antonio and Bassanio

SOLANIO: Companion of Antonio and Bassanio

GRATIANO: Companion of Antonio and Bassanio

BASSANIO: A Venetian gentleman, suitor to Portia

PORTIA: An heiress of Belmont

NERISSA: Portia's waiting-gentlewoman

SHYLOCK: A Jewish moneylender in Venice

PRINCE OF MOROCCO: Suitor to Portia

PRINCE OF ARRAGON: Suitor to Portia

DUKE OF VENICE

LORENZO: Companion of Antonio and Bassanio

JESSICA: Shylock's daughter

CHORUS MEMBERS

NARRATOR

✳ SCENE 1. (ACT II, SCENE II | ACT I, SCENE I)

Venice. A street.

STAGEHANDS *set stools and table downstage center.*

Enter **LANCELET** *from stage left.*

LANCELET
> The fiend is at mine elbow and tempts me
> Saying to me
> "Good Lancelet, use your legs,
> Run away."
> Well my conscience says, "Good Lancelet,
> Budge not."
> "Budge," says the fiend.
> "Budge not," says my conscience.
> To be ruled by my conscience, I should stay
> With the Jew, my master, who (God bless the mark)
> Is a kind of devil, and to run away from the Jew
> I should be ruled by the fiend, who (saving your
>   reverence)
> Is the Devil himself.
> The fiend gives the more friendly counsel.
> I will run, fiend. I will run!
> *(winks, replacing his hat with* **SOLARINO'S** *hat)*

Exit **LANCELET** *stage right.*

Enter **NARRATOR** *from stage rear, coming downstage center.*

NARRATOR

> Bassanio informs his friend Antonio of his love
> for the wealthy Portia, and Antonio offers to loan
> Bassanio some money. (Never a good idea.)

Exit NARRATOR *stage left.*

Enter ANTONIO, SOLANIO, *and* SOLARINO *from stage right.*
ANTONIO *sits on center stool and pours wine into mugs.*

ANTONIO

> In sooth, I know not why I am so sad:
> It wearies me; you say it wearies you;
> And such a want-wit sadness makes of me,
> That I have much ado to know myself.

SOLARINO *(standing and stepping downstage center, gesturing*
> *at imagined ships)*
> Your mind is tossing on the ocean;
> There, where your argosies with portly sail,
> Do overpeer the petty traffickers,
> As they fly by them with their woven wings.
> What harm a wind too great at sea might do.
> I know, Antonio
> Is sad to think upon his merchandise.

ANTONIO

> My ventures are not in one bottom trusted,
> Therefore my merchandise makes me not sad.

SOLANIO

> Then let us say you are sad,
> Because you are not merry.

Exit SOLARINO *and* SOLANIO *stage right. As they exit, they clink*
their mugs together with ANTONIO'S, *greet* BASSANIO *as he enters,*

and sing, "Ciao bella, ciao bella, bella bella ciao ciao."

Enter BASSANIO *from stage right.*

ANTONIO *stands. He and* BASSANIO *greet each other. They sit;*
ANTONIO *pulls his chair closer to* BASSANIO *and leans in.*

ANTONIO *(to* BASSANIO*)*
> Well, tell me now what lady is the same
> To whom you swore a secret pilgrimage?

BASSANIO
> 'Tis not unknown to you, Antonio,
> How much I have disabled mine estate.
> > *(stands and paces)*
> My chief care
> Is to come fairly off from the great debts
> Wherein my time something too prodigal
> Hath left me gaged.

ANTONIO *(stands facing* BASSANIO*)*
> *(earnestly)* Good Bassanio,
> My purse, my person, my extremest means,
> Lie all unlock'd to your occasions.
> Therefore, speak.

BASSANIO *(slowly walks downstage center, envisioning* PORTIA*)*
> In Belmont is a lady richly left;

ANTONIO *sits again, listening intently.*

> And she is fair, and, fairer than that word,
> Of wondrous virtues: sometimes from her eyes
> I did receive fair speechless messages:
> Her name is Portia.
> > *(scowls)* The four winds blow in from every coast

Renowned suitors, *(enchanted smile)* and her
    sunny locks
Hang on her temples like a golden fleece;
    (turns back to ANTONIO, *sits, and pulls*
    his chair close)
O my Antonio, had I but the means
To hold a rival place with one of them.

ANTONIO

Thou know'st that all my fortunes are at sea;
therefore go forth;
Try what my credit can in Venice do:
To furnish thee to Belmont, to fair Portia.

Exit BASSANIO *and* ANTONIO *together stage left, taking wineskin*
and mugs with them.

✳ **SCENE 2.** (ACT I, SCENE II)

Belmont. A room in PORTIA'S *house.*

Enter NARRATOR *from stage rear, coming downstage center.*

NARRATOR

Portia bemoans her late father's rule that she can only be married if one of her suitor's chooses the correct chest of gold, silver, or lead. I wouldn't like that either.

Exit NARRATOR *stage left.*

Enter PORTIA *and* NERISSA *from stage right.* PORTIA *plunks herself into a chair, and* NERISSA *stands behind her, brushing* PORTIA'S *hair.*

PORTIA

By my troth, Nerissa, my little body is aweary of this great world.

NERISSA

You would be, sweet madam, if your miseries were in the same abundance as your good fortunes are.

PORTIA

I may neither choose whom I would nor refuse whom I dislike; so is the will of a living daughter curbed by the will of a dead father.

NERISSA (*sits next to* PORTIA)

> Your father was ever virtuous; therefore the lottery,
> that he hath devised in the three chests of gold,
> silver, and lead, whereof who chooses his meaning
> chooses you, will, no doubt, never be chosen by any
> rightly but one who shall rightly love.
>
> > (*pauses, smiles slyly*)
>
> Do you not remember, lady, in your father's time, a
> Venetian, a scholar and a soldier?

PORTIA (*leaps up*)

> (*excitedly*) Yes, yes, it was Bassanio; (*catches herself
> and sits down as if nothing has happened*) as I think,
> he was so called.

NERISSA (*leans in, giggles*)

> True, madam: he, of all the men that ever my foolish
> eyes looked upon, was the best deserving a fair lady.

PORTIA

> I remember him well, and I remember him worthy
> of thy praise. Come, Nerissa.

Exit PORTIA *and* NERISSA *stage right, laughing excitedly.*

✳ SCENE 3. (ACT I, SCENE III)

Venice. A public place.

Enter **NARRATOR** *from stage rear, coming downstage center.*

NARRATOR
> Antonio borrows money from Shylock the Jew, with a disturbing condition.

Exit **NARRATOR** *stage left.*

Enter **SHYLOCK** *from stage right. He sits on stage right stool and begins reading a newspaper.*

Enter **BASSIANO** *from stage right, following* **SHYLOCK**.

SHYLOCK
> Three thousand ducats; well.

BASSANIO *(standing over* **SHYLOCK***)*
> Ay, sir, for three months.
> For the which, as I told you, Antonio shall be bound.
> Shall I know your answer?

SHYLOCK
> Antonio is sufficient. Yet his means are in supposition: *(points to the newspaper)* He hath an argosy bound to Tripolis, another to the Indies; and other ventures he hath, squandered abroad. But ships are but boards, there is the peril of winds and

rocks. The man is, notwithstanding, sufficient. May I speak with Antonio?

BASSANIO

If it please you to dine with us.

SHYLOCK

Yes, to smell pork; to eat of the habitation which your prophet the Nazarite conjured the devil into. I will buy with you, sell with you, but I will not eat with you. Who is he comes here?

Enter **ANTONIO** *from stage right.*

BASSANIO

This is Signior Antonio.

BASSIANO *crosses stage right to greet* **ANTONIO**.

SHYLOCK *(stands and takes a step toward audience)*
        (aside) I hate him for he is a Christian,
        But more for he lends out money gratis and
                brings down
        The rate of usance here with us in Venice.
        He hates our sacred nation, and he rails
        On me, my bargains, and my well-won thrift,
        Which he calls interest. Cursed be my tribe,
        If I forgive him!

ANTONIO *and* **BASSANIO** *return to stage left.*

        (to **ANTONIO***)* Rest you fair, good signior.

ANTONIO, **BASSANIO**, *and* **SHYLOCK** *sit.*

ANTONIO

Shylock, although I neither lend nor borrow

Yet, to supply the ripe wants of my friend,
I'll break a custom.
Shall we be beholding to you?

SHYLOCK *(leans in toward* **ANTONIO***)*
Signior Antonio, many a time and oft
In the Rialto you have rated me
About my moneys and my usances:
Still have I borne it with a patient shrug,
For sufferance is the badge of all our tribe.
You call me misbeliever, cut-throat dog,
And spit upon my Jewish gaberdine,
Well then, it now appears you need my help:
Fair sir, you spit on me on Wednesday last;
You call'd me dog; and for these courtesies
I'll lend you thus much moneys?

SHYLOCK *sits and picks up his newspaper, bringing it up to his face.*

ANTONIO *(stands and grabs newspaper away from* **SHYLOCK***,*
throwing it to the ground)
I am as like to call thee so again,
To spit on thee again.

SHYLOCK *stares at* **ANTONIO***, picks up newspaper slowly, and smiles coldly. He folds newspaper and sets it on stool, laughs coldly, and stands.*

SHYLOCK
Why, look you, how you storm!
Go with me to a notary, seal me there
Your single bond; and, in a merry sport,
If you repay me not on such a day,
Let the forfeit
Be nominated for an equal pound

Of your fair flesh, to be cut off and taken
In what part of your body pleaseth me.

BASSANIO *(stands urgently and takes* ANTONIO *by the shoulders)*
You shall not seal to such a bond for me.

ANTONIO *(quietly to* BASSANIO*)*
Why, fear not, man; I will not forfeit it:
(to SHYLOCK*)* Yes Shylock, I will seal unto this bond.

SHYLOCK *pauses and then extends his hand for* ANTONIO *to
shake.* BASSANIO *and* SHYLOCK *exchange a glance.* ANTONIO
shakes SHYLOCK'S *hand.*

SHYLOCK
Then meet me forthwith at the notary's.

ANTONIO
Hie thee, gentle Jew.

Exit SHYLOCK *stage left.*

(cheerfully, but with an edge in his voice)
The Hebrew will turn Christian: He grows kind.

BASSANIO *(dismayed and worried)*
I like not fair terms and a villain's mind.

ANTONIO
Come on: In this there can be no dismay;
My ships come home a month before the day.

Exit ANTONIO *stage left.*

Exit BASSANIO *stage left, glancing worriedly at the horizon.*

✳ SCENE 4. (ACT II, SCENE I | ACT II, SCENE VII)

Belmont. A room in **PORTIA'S** *house.*

STAGEHANDS *set stools on either side of table at center stage to form a straight line and set caskets on top.*

Enter **NARRATOR** *from stage rear, coming downstage center.*

NARRATOR
> The Prince of Morocco tries his luck at picking
> the right chest to win Portia's hand.
> *(afterthought, while exiting)* Good luck!

Exit **NARRATOR** *stage left.*

Enter **PORTIA** *and* **NERISSA** *from stage right.*

Drumbeats with a dance rhythm sound from offstage.

Enter the **PRINCE OF MOROCCO** *with* **CHORUS** *dancing in behind him.*

MOROCCO
> Mislike me not for my complexion,
> The shadow'd livery of the burnish'd sun,
> I would not change this hue,
> Except to steal your thoughts, my gentle queen.

PORTIA

You must take your chance,
And either not attempt to choose at all
Or swear before you choose, if you choose wrong
Never to speak to lady afterward
In way of marriage: Therefore be advised.

MOROCCO

Good fortune then!
To make me blest or cursed among men.

PORTIA

Go draw aside the curtains, noble prince.
Now make your choice.

MOROCCO *draws the curtains with a flourish.* **CHORUS** *echoes*
MOROCCO'S *movement.*

MOROCCO

How shall I know if I do choose the right?

PORTIA

The one of them contains my picture, prince:
If you choose that, then I am yours withal.

MOROCCO *looks up, making upward gesture with arms.* **CHORUS**
repeats this movement.

MOROCCO

Some god direct my judgment! *(looks at lead casket)*
Let me see;
What says this leaden casket?
(to audience) "Who chooseth me must give
and hazard all he hath."
I'll then nor give nor hazard aught for lead.
(looks at silver casket)

What says the silver with her virgin hue?
"Who chooseth me shall get as much as he deserves."
I do in birth deserve her, and in fortunes.
Let's see once more this saying graved in gold
"Who chooseth me shall gain what many men desire."
Why, that's the lady; all the world desires her;
One of these three contains her heavenly picture.
    (looks at gold casket)
Here an angel in a golden bed
Lies all within. Deliver me the key:
Here do I choose, and thrive I as I may!

PORTIA *(gives key to* **MOROCCO***)*
    There, take it, prince; and if my form lie there,
    Then I am yours.

Drumroll sounds from offstage. **MOROCCO** *unlocks the gold casket and pulls out a prop skull with a rolled up piece of paper in it.*

MOROCCO *laughs heartily as* **CHORUS** *laughs behind him.* **MOROCCO** *then screams, and* **CHORUS** *echoes* **MOROCCO'S** *scream.*

MOROCCO
    O hell! What have we here?
    A carrion Death, within whose empty eye
    There is a written scroll! I'll read the writing.

MOROCCO *shows scroll to* **CHORUS***. They mime putting on monocles to examine the scroll.*

Drumroll sounds from offstage.

CHORUS
    "All that glitters is not gold;
    Often have you heard that told:

Gilded tombs do worms enfold.
Fare you well; your suit is cold."
Cold, indeed; and labor lost:
Then, farewell, heat, and welcome, frost!
Portia, adieu. I have too grieved a heart
To take a tedious leave: Thus losers part.

Drumbeats with a dance rhythm sound from offstage.

Exit MOROCCO *stage left with* CHORUS *behind him, dancing despondently.*

Drumming stops.

PORTIA

A gentle riddance. Draw the curtains, go. Let all of his complexion choose me so.

Drumbeats with a dance rhythm sound from offstage.

Exit PORTIA *and* NERISSA *stage left, dancing like* MOROCCO *and* CHORUS.

✳ **SCENE 5.** (ACT II, SCENE IX)

Belmont. A room in **PORTIA'S** *house.*

Enter **NARRATOR** *from stage rear, coming downstage center.*

NARRATOR

> Next up is the Prince of Arragon. Will he fare any
> better? Place your bets.

Exit **NARRATOR** *stage left.*

Enter **NERISSA** *and* **PORTIA** *from stage left.*

NERISSA

> Quick, quick, I pray thee; draw the curtain straight:
> The Prince of Arragon hath ta'en his oath,
> And comes to his election presently.

Drumbeats with a dance rhythm sound from offstage.

Enter the **PRINCE OF ARRAGON** *and his* **CHORUS** *from stage right, dancing.*

PORTIA

> Behold, there stand the caskets, noble prince:
> If you choose that wherein I am contain'd,
> Straight shall our nuptial rites be solemnized:
> But if you fail, without more speech, my lord,
> You must be gone from hence immediately.

ARRAGON
> Fortune now
> To my heart's hope! Gold, silver, and base lead.
> *(to audience)* "Who chooseth me must give
>   and hazard all he hath."
> You shall look fairer, ere I give or hazard.

ARRAGON *laughs a silly laugh at his own joke.* **CHORUS** *echoes his laugh.*

PORTIA *and* **NERISSA** *exchange a look.*

> What says the golden chest? Ha! Let me see:
> *(to audience)* "Who chooseth me shall gain what
>   many men desire."
> That "many" may be meant by the fool multitude.
> Why, then to thee, thou silver treasure-house;
> *(to audience)* "Who chooseth me shall get as much
>   as he deserves."
> I will assume desert. Give me a key for this,
> And instantly unlock my fortunes here.

Drumroll sounds from offstage.

ARRAGON *opens the silver casket and pulls out a doll or bust of a fool's head.*

ARRAGON
> What's here? The portrait of a blinking idiot,
> Did I deserve no more than a fool's head?
> What is here?

Drumroll sounds from offstage.

CHORUS
> "Some there be that shadows kiss;
> Such have but a shadow's bliss:

I will ever be your head:
So be gone: You are sped."
With one fool's head I came to woo,
But I go away with two.
Sweet, adieu. I'll keep my oath,
Patiently to bear my *(pauses, makes a face)* wroth?

Exit ARRAGON *and* CHORUS *stage right, giving dismissive waves, while drumbeats sound from offstage.*

Drumming stops.

PORTIA

Thus hath the candle singed the moth.
O, these deliberate fools!

Exit PORTIA *and* NERISSA *stage left, imitating* ARRAGON, *while drumbeats resume from offstage.*

✳ **SCENE 6.** (ACT III, SCENE II)

Belmont. A room in PORTIA'S *house.*

Enter NARRATOR *from stage rear, coming downstage center.*

NARRATOR
>Portia's final suitor is Bassanio. *(whispers)* I'm
>rooting for this guy.

Exit NARRATOR *stage left.*

Enter PORTIA *and* NERISSA *from stage left.*

PORTIA
>Come, Nerissa; for I long to see
>Quick Cupid's post that comes so mannerly.

NERISSA *(looks excitedly stage left)*
>Bassanio, lord Love, if thy will it be!

Enter BASSANIO *from stage left, as drumbeats with a dance rhythm sound from offstage.* CHORUS *(including* GRATIANO*) follows behind him, dancing and drumming.* BASSANIO *stops and turns around threateningly, and* CHORUS *all bump into each other and scurry to their places.*

PORTIA *(touches* BASSANIO'S *sleeve)*
>I pray you, tarry: Pause a day or two
>Before you hazard; for, in choosing wrong,
>I lose your company: Therefore forbear awhile.
>*(looks in his eyes)* Beshrew your eyes,

(*turns away toward audience*) They have o'erlook'd
me and divided me;
One half of me is yours, the other half (*pauses,
looks to* BASSANIO, *and then looks back to
audience, smiling*) yours.

BASSANIO (*looks into* PORTIA'S *eyes, then turns to look at caskets*)
Let me choose
For as I am, I live upon the rack.
(*mimes being tortured*)
(*quickly turns toward caskets*) But let me to my
fortune and the caskets.

PORTIA (*steps back to give* BASSANIO *room to look at caskets*)
Away, then! I am lock'd in one of them:
If you do love me, you will find me out.
Let music sound while he doth make his choice.

Drumbeats from offstage accompany music.

CHORUS
Tell me where is fancy bred,
Or in the heart, or in the head?
How begot, how nourished?
Reply, reply.
It is engender'd in the eyes,
With gazing fed; and fancy dies
In the cradle where it lies.
Let us all ring fancy's knell
I'll begin it—Ding, dong, bell.

BASSANIO
The world is still deceived with ornament.
(*examines gold casket*) Therefore, thou gaudy gold,
Hard food for Midas, I will none of thee;
(*examines silver casket*) Nor none of thee, thou pale

and common drudge
'Tween man and man: but thou, thou meager lead
(*picks up lead casket*)
Thy paleness moves me more than eloquence;
And here choose I; joy be the consequence!

Drumroll sounds from offstage.

CHORUS *leans forward in anticipation.*

What find I here?
(*opens the lead casket and holds up photo of* **PORTIA**)
Fair Portia's counterfeit! What demi-god
Hath come so near creation? Move these eyes?
Seem they in motion? Here are sever'd lips,
Parted with sugar breath. (*sniffs the air*)
Here's the scroll,
The continent and summary of my fortune.

BASSANIO *shows scroll to* **CHORUS**, *who mime taking out monocles to read it.*

Drumroll sounds from offstage.

CHORUS (*illustrating words with movement*)
"You that choose not by the view,
Chance as fair and choose as true!
Turn you where your lady is
And claim her with a loving kiss."

CHORUS *leans forward to see if* **BASSANIO** *will kiss* **PORTIA**.
BASSANIO *kisses* **PORTIA** *on the cheek.* **CHORUS** *coos happily.*

PORTIA
You see me, Lord Bassanio, where I stand,
Such as I am.

Happiest of all is that her gentle spirit
Commits itself to yours.

PORTIA *turns her cheek for* BASSANIO *to kiss. When he gets close,*
she turns again and kisses him on the lips.

BASSANIO *(stunned)*
Madam, you have bereft me of all words,
Only my blood speaks, to you in my veins.

NERISSA
Good joy, my lord and lady!

During the previous moments, NERISSA *and* GRATIANO *have*
been eyeing each other and inching closer together. They are
now side by side.

GRATIANO
I may be married too.
(*holds* NERISSA'S *hand*)
I got a promise of this fair one here
(*gazes at her lovingly*)
To have her love, provided that your fortune
Achieved her mistress.

PORTIA *(amazed and overjoyed)*
Is this true, Nerissa?

NERISSA
Madam, it is.

BASSANIO *(troubled and agitated; begins to pace downstage)*
O sweet Portia,
When I told you
My state was nothing, I should then have told you
That I was worse than nothing; for, indeed,

(looks out, as if looking over the troubled seas)
I have engaged myself to a dear friend.

PORTIA *(walks toward him and puts her hand on his shoulder)*
Is it your dear friend that is thus in trouble?

BASSANIO *nods.*

What sum owes he the Jew?

BASSANIO
For me three thousand ducats.

PORTIA *(unfazed)*
What, no more?

PORTIA *snaps her fingers, and each of the six* **CHORUS** *members holds out a bag of money.* **PORTIA** *snaps her fingers again, and one* **CHORUS** *member holds out a large bag. All other* **CHORUS** *members drop their bag of money in large bag.* **CHORUS** *member hands large bag to* **PORTIA**, *who hands the bag to* **BASSANIO**.

Pay him six thousand, and deface the bond.

BASSANIO
Since I have your good leave to go away,
I will make haste.

Drumbeats from offstage play a love song as couples dance offstage two by two in a conga line.

Exit **ALL** *stage right,* **CHORUS** *members taking caskets with them.* **ALL** *continue dancing as they exit.*

✳ **SCENE 7.** (ACT IV, SCENE I)

Venice. A court of justice.

Enter **NARRATOR** *from stage rear, coming downstage center.*

NARRATOR
> In the courtroom, Shylock arrives to claim his
> pound of flesh from Antonio. *(whispers)* There is a
> mystery guest.

Exit **NARRATOR** *stage left.*

Enter **DUKE, ANTONIO,** *and* **BASSANIO** *from stage right.*

Drumbeats with a dance rhythm sound from offstage.

Enter **CHORUS** *from stage right, drumming and dancing.*

DUKE *(stands)*
> *(yells)* Silence!

CHORUS *members stop and scurry to their positions.*

DUKE *sits on center stool and* **ANTONIO** *sits on stage left stool.*

DUKE
> Antonio, I am sorry for thee: Thou art come to answer
> an inhuman wretch, void and empty
> From any dram of mercy.

ANTONIO

> I am arm'd
> To suffer, with a quietness of spirit,
> The very tyranny and rage of his.

DUKE

> Go one, and call the Jew into the court.

Exit one **CHORUS** *member stage right to retrieve* **SHYLOCK.**

Enter **SHYLOCK** *from stage right, holding a scroll of rolled-up paper: his bond. He sits on stage right stool.*

DUKE *(stands)*

> *(with authority)* Shylock, the world thinks, and I
>   think so too,
> That thou but lead'st this fashion of thy malice
> To the last hour of act; and then 'tis thought
> Thou'lt show thy mercy and remorse more strange
> Than is thy strange apparent cruelty;
> We all expect a gentle answer, Jew.

SHYLOCK *(stands)*

> By our holy Sabbath have I sworn
> To have the due and forfeit of my bond:
> I give no reason, nor I will not,
> More than a lodged hate and a certain loathing
> I bear Antonio.
> Are you answer'd?

CHORUS *answers, "No!" and general pandemonium follows.*

BASSANIO *(angrily steps toward* **SHYLOCK***)*

> This is no answer, thou unfeeling man.
> For thy three thousand ducats here is six.
>   *(hands* **SHYLOCK** *bag of money)*

SHYLOCK *looks into the bag, swallows hard, and drops it at* BASSANIO'S *feet.* CHORUS *utters, "Ooh!" in response.*

SHYLOCK
> If every ducat in six thousand ducats
> Were in six parts and every part a ducat,
> *(very distinctly)* I would not draw them; I would
> have my bond.

DUKE *(still standing)*
> How shalt thou hope for mercy, rendering none?

SHYLOCK *(walks downstage right, away from the others)*
> What judgment shall I dread, doing no wrong?
> You have among you many a purchased slave,
> Which, like your asses and your dogs and mules,
> You use in abject and in slavish parts,
> Because you bought them.
> The pound of flesh, which I demand of him,
> Is dearly bought; 'tis mine and *(distinctly)* I will have it.

SHYLOCK *takes out knife and* CHORUS *cries, "No!"*

Enter SOLARINO *from stage right.*

SOLARINO
> My lord, here stays without
> A messenger with letters from the doctor,
> New come from Padua.

DUKE
> Bring us the letter; call the messenger.

Exit SOLARINO *stage right to retrieve* NERISSA.

Enter NERISSA *from stage right, dressed as a lawyer's clerk. She bows to* DUKE.

DUKE

    Came you from Padua, from Bellario?

NERISSA

    From both, my lord. Bellario greets your grace.

NERISSA *presents a letter to* DUKE. DUKE *reads the letter to himself.*

DUKE

    This letter from Bellario doth commend
    A young and learned doctor to our court.
    Where is he?

NERISSA

    He attendeth here hard by. *(points stage right)*

Enter PORTIA *from stage right, dressed as a doctor of laws.*

DUKE

    And here, I take it, is the doctor come.
    Give me your hand. Come you from old Bellario?

PORTIA *comes center, starts to curtsy but catches herself, and then bows to* DUKE. *Meanwhile,* SHYLOCK *walks upstage to sit on stage right stool.*

PORTIA

    I did, my lord.
    I am informed thoroughly of the cause.
    Which is the merchant here, and which the Jew?

SHYLOCK *(stands)*

    Shylock is my name.

PORTIA

(*to* ANTONIO) You stand within his danger,
　　do you not?

ANTONIO (*stands*)

Ay, so he says.

PORTIA

Do you confess the bond?

ANTONIO

I do.

PORTIA

Then must the Jew be merciful.

SHYLOCK (*animated and agitated*)

On what compulsion must I? Tell me that.

PORTIA *gestures for* SHYLOCK *to sit;* SHYLOCK *sits.*

PORTIA

(*to* SHYLOCK) The quality of mercy is not strain'd,
(*moves downstage and talks out over audience*)
It droppeth as the gentle rain from heaven
Upon the place beneath: it is twice blest;
It blesseth him that gives and him that takes.

SHYLOCK (*stands, agitated*)

My deeds upon my head! I crave the law,
The penalty and forfeit of my bond.

PORTIA

I pray you, let me look upon the bond.
(*takes bond from* SHYLOCK)
Why, this bond is forfeit;

> And lawfully by this the Jew may claim
> A pound of flesh, to be by him cut off
> Nearest the merchant's heart.

PORTIA *kneels at* **SHYLOCK'S** *chair and softly pleads with him.*

> Be merciful:
> Take twice thy money; bid me tear the bond.

SHYLOCK *(stares at* **PORTIA***)*
> *(firmly)* There is no power in the tongue of man
> To alter me: I stay here on my bond.

PORTIA
> Why then, thus it is:
> *(hands the paper back to* **SHYLOCK** *and turns to*
> **ANTONIO***)*
> You must prepare your bosom for his knife.

DUKE *motions two* **BAILIFFS** *to stand over* **ANTONIO.**

They do so, with **BASSANIO** *acting threatening toward* **BAILIFFS** *by standing between them and* **ANTONIO.**

DUKE *waves* **BASSANIO** *back.*

SHYLOCK
> We trifle time: I pray thee, pursue sentence.

Dramatic drumbeat sounds from offstage.

SHYLOCK *sharpens his knife and approaches* **ANTONIO.** **CHORUS** *murmurs and grows noisy. As* **SHYLOCK** *draws close, he brings knife up over his head.* **CHORUS** *gasps.*

PORTIA
> Tarry a little; *(* **PORTIA** *moves between* **SHYLOCK** *and*

ANTONIO) there is something else.
This bond doth give thee here no jot of blood;
The words expressly are "a pound of flesh:"
Take then thy bond, take thou thy pound of flesh;
But, in the cutting it, if thou dost shed
One drop of Christian blood, thy lands and goods
Are, by the laws of Venice, confiscate
Unto the state of Venice.

SHYLOCK
Is that the law?

PORTIA
Thyself shalt see the act:

PORTIA *shows* SHYLOCK *the passage in the book. He examines it carefully.*

For, as thou urgest justice, be assured
Thou shalt have justice, more than thou desirest.
Therefore prepare thee to cut off the flesh.
Shed thou no blood, nor cut thou less nor more
But just a pound of flesh: If the scale do turn
But in the estimation of a hair,
Thou diest and all thy goods are confiscate.

SHYLOCK *(incredulous and stunned)*
(sits) Give me my principal, and let me go.

SHYLOCK *returns book to* PORTIA *and holds his hand out for the money.*

PORTIA
Thou shalt have nothing but the forfeiture,
To be so taken at thy peril, Jew.

ALL *whisper, "Jew."*

SHYLOCK
> I'll stay no longer. *(stands)*

PORTIA
> Tarry, Jew:

PORTIA *motions for* SHYLOCK *to sit down; he refuses.*

ALL *repeat, "Jew," louder and point.* SHYLOCK *sits.*

> The law hath yet another hold on you.
> It is enacted in the laws of Venice,
> If it be proved against an alien

CHORUS *says, "Jew!" more loudly and points.*

> That by direct or indirect attempts
> He seek the life of any citizen,
> The party 'gainst the which he doth contrive
> Shall seize one half his goods; the other half
> Comes to the privy coffer of the state;
> And the offender's life lies in the mercy
> Of the duke only.
> Down therefore and beg mercy of the duke.
> > *(points for* SHYLOCK *to kneel)*

SHYLOCK *refuses.* ALL *repeat, "Down."* SHYLOCK *kneels.*

DUKE
> That thou shalt see the difference of our spirits,
> I pardon thee thy life before thou ask it:
> For half thy wealth, it is Antonio's;
> The other half comes to the general state.

SHYLOCK

Nay, take my life and all; pardon not that:
You take my life
When you do take the means whereby I live.

PORTIA

What mercy can you render him, Antonio?

ANTONIO

So please my lord the Duke and all the court
To quit the fine for one half of his goods,
I am content; More, that, for this favor,
He presently become a Christian

PORTIA

Art thou contented, Jew? What dost thou say?

SHYLOCK (*defeated*)

I am content.
I pray you, give me leave to go from hence;
I am not well.

DUKE

Get thee gone.

Exit **SHYLOCK** *stage right.*

PORTIA (*to* **BASSANIO,** *mysteriously, with a hint of a smile*)

I pray you, know me when we meet again:
I wish you well, and so I take my leave.

BASSANIO *appears puzzled by* **PORTIA'S** *words.*

Military drumbeat sounds from offstage.

ALL *exit stage left, somberly.*

✳ **SCENE 8.** (ACT V, SCENE I)

Belmont. Avenue to PORTIA'S *house.*

Enter NARRATOR *from stage rear, coming downstage center.*

NARRATOR
> All secrets are revealed. Because this is a comedy,
> everybody ends up happy. Except Shylock. Which is
> kind of a big "except." *(shrugs)* Enjoy!

Exit NARRATOR *stage left.*

Enter LORENZO *from stage right and* JESSICA *from stage left, walking toward each other.*

LORENZO
> The moon shines bright: in such a night as this,
> When the sweet wind did gently kiss the trees.
> In such a night
> Did Jessica steal from the wealthy Jew
> And with an unthrift love did run from Venice
> As far as Belmont.

LORENZO *and* JESSICA *meet at center stage and join hands.*

JESSICA
> In such a night
> Did young Lorenzo swear he loved her well,
> Stealing her soul with many vows of faith *(unclasps*
> > *his hands and in a playful snub, turns away)*
> And ne'er a true one.

LORENZO *(plays along as if he is insulted and also turns away)*
> In such a night
> Did pretty Jessica, like a little shrew,
> Slander her love,

JESSICA *and* **LORENZO** *both look over their shoulders at each other and smile.*

> and he forgave her.

JESSICA *and* **LORENZO** *turn back to each other, hug, and laugh.*

Enter **PORTIA** *and* **NERISSA** *from stage right, still dressed as a lawyer and clerk, ready to surprise their husbands.*

LORENZO *(hearing approaching footsteps stage right)*
> *(to* **PORTIA***)* Your husband is at hand.

Enter quickly **BASSANIO, ANTONIO,** *and* **GRATIANO** *from stage right.*

PORTIA
> You are welcome home, my lord.

BASSANIO
> I thank you . . .?

BASSANIO *and* **GRATIANO** *are both stunned and confused.*

Finally, **PORTIA** *takes off the robe and hat to reveal herself.* **NERISSA** *does the same.*

PORTIA
> You are all amazed:
> Portia was the doctor,
> Nerissa there her clerk.

ANTONIO
>I am dumb.

BASSANIO (*holds* PORTIA'S *hand and laughs*)
>Were you the doctor and I knew you not?

GRATIANO (*also laughing*)
>Were you the clerk?

NERISSA *nods her head and laughs.*

BASSANIO
>Sweet doctor, you shall be my bed-fellow:
>When I am absent, then lie with (*looks around,*
>>*points back to* PORTIA) my wife.

NERISSA (*to* LORENZO)
>There do I give to you and Jessica,
>From the rich Jew, a special deed of gift,
>After his death, of all he dies possess'd of.

NERISSA *hands* LORENZO *a piece of paper.*

LORENZO
>Fair ladies, you drop manna in the way
>Of starved people.

ALL *stand side by side as couples, facing the audience and smiling.*

PORTIA
>Let us go in;
>and we will answer all things faithfully.

Enter ALL.

ALL *(unison)*

> I am a Jew. Hath not a Jew eyes? Hath not a Jew
> hands, senses, affections, passions? Fed with the
> same food, hurt with the same weapons, subject
> to the same diseases, healed by the same means,
> warmed and cooled by the same winter and
> summer, as a Christian is? If you prick us, do we not
> bleed? and if you wrong us, shall we not revenge?

ALL *hold hands and take a bow. Exeunt.*

* PERFORMING SHAKESPEARE

HOW *THE 30-MINUTE SHAKESPEARE* WAS BORN

In 1981 I performed a "Shakespeare Juggling" piece called "To Juggle or Not To Juggle" at the first Folger Library Secondary School Shakespeare Festival. The audience consisted of about 200 Washington, D.C. area high school students who had just performed thirty-minute versions of Shakespeare plays for each other and were jubilant over the experience. I was dressed in a jester's outfit, and my job was to entertain them. I juggled and jested and played with Shakespeare's words, notably Hamlet's "To be or not to be" soliloquy, to very enthusiastic response. I was struck by how much my "Shakespeare Juggling" resonated with a group who had just performed Shakespeare themselves. "Getting" Shakespeare is a heady feeling, especially for adolescents, and I am continually delighted at how much joy and satisfaction young people derive from performing Shakespeare. Simply reading and studying this great playwright does not even come close to inspiring the kind of enthusiasm that comes from performance.

Surprisingly, many of these students were not "actor types." A good percentage of the students performing Shakespeare that day were part of an English class which had rehearsed the plays during class time. Fifteen years later, when I first started directing plays in D.C. public schools as a Teaching Artist with the Folger Shakespeare Library, I entered a ninth grade English class as a guest and spent two or three days a week for two or three months preparing students for the Folger's annual Secondary School Shakespeare Festival. I have conducted this annual residency with the Folger ever since. Every year for seven action-packed days, eight groups of students between grades seven and twelve tread the boards onstage at the Folger's Elizabethan Theatre, a grand recreation of a sixteenth-century venue with a three-tiered gallery, carved oak columns, and a sky-painted canopy.

As noted on the Folger website (www.folger.edu), "The festival is a celebration of the Bard, not a competition. Festival commentators—drawn from the professional theater and Shakespeare education communities—recognize exceptional performances, student directors, and good spirit amongst the students with selected awards at the end of each day. They are also available to share feedback with the students."

My annual Folger Teaching Artist engagement, directing a Shakespeare play in a public high school English class, is the most challenging and the most rewarding thing I do all year. I hope this book can bring you the same rewards.

GETTING STARTED

GAMES

How can you get an English class (or any other group of young people, or even adults) to start the seemingly daunting task of performing a Shakespeare play? You have already successfully completed the critical first step, which is buying this book. You hold in your hand a performance-ready, thirty-minute cutting of a Shakespeare play, with stage directions to get the actors moving about the stage purposefully. But it's a good idea to warm the group up with some theater games.

One good initial exercise is called "Positive/Negative Salutations." Students stand in two lines facing each other (four or five students in each line) and, reading from index cards, greet each other, first with a "Positive" salutation in Shakespeare's language (using actual phrases from the plays), followed by a "negative" greeting.

Additionally, short vocal exercises are an essential part of the preparation process. The following is a very simple and effective vocal warm-up: Beginning with the number two, have the whole group count to twenty using increments of two (i.e., "Two, four, six . . ."). Increase the volume slightly with each number, reaching top volume with "twenty," and then decrease the volume while counting back down, so that the students are practically whispering when they arrive again at "two." This exercise teaches dynamics and allows them to get loud as a group without any individual pressure. Frequently during a rehearsal period, if a student is mumbling inaudibly, I will refer back to this exercise as a reminder that we can and often do belt it out!

"Stomping Words" is a game that is very helpful at getting a handle on Shakespeare's rhythm. Choose a passage in iambic pentameter and have the group members walk around the room in a circle, stomping their feet on the second beat of each line:

Two **house**-holds, **both** a-**like** in **dig**-nity
In **fair** Ve-**ro**na **Where** we **lay** our **scene**

Do the same thing with a prose passage, and have the students discuss their experience with it, including points at which there is an extra beat, etc., and what, if anything, it might signify.

I end every vocal warm-up with a group reading of one of the speeches from the play, emphasizing diction and projection, bouncing off consonants, and encouraging the group members to listen to each other so that they can speak the lines together in unison. For variety I will throw in some classic "tongue twisters" too, such as, "The sixth sheik's sixth sheep is sick."

The Folger Shakespeare Library's website (http://www.folger.edu) and their book series *Shakespeare Set Free*, edited by Peggy O'Brien, are two great resources for getting started with a performance-based teaching of Shakespeare in the classroom. The Folger website has numerous helpful resources and activities, many submitted by teachers, for helping a class actively participate in the process of getting to know a Shakespeare play. For more simple theater games, Viola Spolin's *Theatre Games for the Classroom* is very helpful, as is one I use frequently, *Theatre Games for Young Performers.*

HATS AND PROPS

Introducing a few hats and props early in the process is a good way to get the action going. Hats, in particular, provide a nice avenue for giving young actors a non-verbal way of getting into character. In the opening weeks, when students are still holding onto their scripts, a hat can give an actor a way to "feel" like a character. Young actors are natural masters at injecting their own personality into what they wear, and even small choices made with how a hat is worn (jauntily, shadily, cockily, mysteriously) provide a starting point for discussion of specific characters, their traits, and their relationships with other characters. All such discussions always lead back to one thing: the text. "Mining the text" is consistently the best strategy for uncovering the mystery of Shakespeare's language. That is where all the answers lie: in the words themselves.

WHAT DO THE WORDS MEAN?

It is essential that young actors know what they are saying when they recite Shakespeare. If not, they might as well be scat singing, riffing on sounds and rhythm but not conveying a specific meaning. The real question is: What do the words mean? The answer is multifaceted, and can be found in more than one place. The New Folger Library paperback editions of the plays themselves (edited by Barbara Mowat and Paul Werstine, Washington Square Press) are a great resource for understanding Shakespeare's words and passages and "translating" them into modern English. These editions also contain chapters on Shakespeare's language, his life, his theater, a "Modern Perspective," and further reading. There is a wealth of scholarship embedded in these wonderful books, and I make it a point to read them cover to cover before embarking on a play-directing project. At the very least, it is a good idea for any adult who intends to direct a Shakespeare play with a group of students to go through the explanatory notes that appear on the pages facing the text. These explanatory notes are an indispensable "translation tool."

The best way to get students to understand what Shakespeare's words mean is to ask them what they think they mean. Students have their own associations with the words and with how they sound and feel. The best ideas on how to perform Shakespeare often come directly from the students, not from anybody else's notion. If a student has an idea or feeling about a word or passage, and it resonates with her emotionally, physically, or spiritually, then Shakespeare's words can be a vehicle for her feelings. That can result in some powerful performances!

I make it my job as director to read the explanatory notes in the Folger text, but I make it clear to the students that almost "anything goes" when trying to understand Shakespeare. There are no wrong interpretations. Students have their own experiences, with some shared and some uniquely their own. If someone has an association with the phrase "canker-blossom," or if the words make that student or his character feel or act a certain way, then that is the "right" way to decipher it.

I encourage the students to refer to the Folger text's explanatory notes and to keep a pocket dictionary handy. Young actors must attach some meaning to every word or line they recite. If I feel an actor is glossing over a word, I will stop him and ask him what he is saying. If he doesn't know, we will figure it out together as a group.

PROCESS VS. PRODUCT

The process of learning Shakespeare by performing one of his plays is more important than whether everybody remembers his lines or whether somebody misses a cue or an entrance. But my Teaching Artist residencies have always had the end goal of a public performance for about 200 other students, so naturally the performance starts to take precedence over the process somewhere around dress rehearsal in the students' minds. It is my job to make sure the actors are prepared—otherwise they will remember the embarrassing moment of a public mistake and not the glorious triumph of owning a Shakespeare play.

In one of my earlier years of play directing, I was sitting in the audience as one of my narrators stood frozen on stage for at least a minute, trying to remember her opening line. I started scrambling in my backpack below my seat for a script, at last prompting her from the audience. Despite her fine performance, that embarrassing moment is all she remembered from the whole experience. Since then I have made sure to assign at least one person to prompt from backstage if necessary. Additionally, I inform the entire cast that if somebody is dying alone out there, it is okay to rescue him or her with an offstage prompt.

There is always a certain amount of stage fright that will accompany a performance, especially a public one for an unfamiliar audience. As a director, I live with stage fright as well, even though I am not appearing on stage. The only antidote to this is work and preparation. If a young actor is struggling with her lines, I make sure to arrange for a session where we run lines over the telephone. I try to set up a buddy system so that students can run lines with their peers, and this often works well. But if somebody does not have a "buddy," I will personally make the time to help out myself. As I assure my students from the outset, I am not going to let them fail or embarrass themselves. They need an experienced leader. And if the leader has experience in teaching but not in directing Shakespeare, then he needs this book!

It is a good idea to culminate in a public performance, as opposed to an in-class project, even if it is only for another classroom. Student actors want to show their newfound Shakespearian thespian skills to an outside group, and this goal motivates them to do a good job. In that respect, "product" is important. Another wonderful bonus to performing a play is that it is a unifying group effort. Students learn teamwork. They learn to give focus to another actor when he is speaking, and to play off of other characters. I like to end each performance with the entire cast reciting a passage in unison. This is a powerful ending, one that reaffirms the unity of the group.

SEEING SHAKESPEARE PERFORMED

It is very helpful for young actors to see Shakespeare performed by a group of professionals, whether they are appearing live on stage (preferable but not always possible) or on film. Because an entire play can take up two or more full class periods, time may be an issue. I am fortunate because thanks to a local foundation that underwrites theater education in the schools, I have been able to take my school groups to a Folger Theatre matinee of the play that they are performing. I always pick a play that is being performed locally that season. But not all group leaders are that lucky. Fortunately, there is the Internet, specifically YouTube. A quick YouTube search for "Shakespeare" can unearth thousands of results, many appropriate for the classroom.

The first "Hamlet" result showed an 18-year-old African-American actor on the streets of Camden, New Jersey, delivering a riveting performance of Hamlet's "The play's the thing." The second clip was from *Cat Head Theatre,* an animation of cats performing Hamlet. Of course, YouTube boasts not just alley cats and feline thespians, but also clips by true legends of the stage, such as John Gielgud and Richard Burton. These clips can be saved and shown in classrooms, providing useful inspiration.

One advantage of the amazing variety of clips available on YouTube is that students can witness the wide range of interpretations for any given scene, speech, or character in Shakespeare, thus freeing them from any preconceived notion that there is a "right" way to do it. Furthermore, modern interpretations of the Bard may appeal to those who are put off by the "thees and thous" of Elizabethan speech.

By seeing Shakespeare performed either live or on film, students are able to hear the cadence, rhythm, vocal dynamics, and pronunciation of the language, and they can appreciate the life that other actors breathe into the characters. They get to see the story told dramatically, which inspires them to tell their own version.

PUTTING IT ALL TOGETHER

THE STEPS

After a few sessions of theater games to warm up the group, it's time to begin the process of casting the play. Each play cutting in *The 30-Minute Shakespeare* series includes a cast list and a sample program, demonstrating which parts have been divided. Cast size is generally between twelve and thirty students, with major roles frequently assigned to more than one performer. In other words, one student may play Juliet in the first scene, another in the second scene, and yet another in the third. This will distribute the parts evenly so that there is no "star of the show." Furthermore, this prevents actors from being burdened with too many lines. If I have an actor who is particularly talented or enthusiastic, I will give her a bigger role. It is important to go with the grain—one cast member's enthusiasm can be contagious.

I provide the performer of each shared role with a similar head-piece and/or cape, so that the audience can keep track of the characters. When there are sets of twins, I try to use blue shirts and red shirts, so that the audience has at least a fighting chance of figuring it out! Other than these costume consistencies, I rely on the text and the audience's observance to sort out the doubling of characters. Generally, the audience can follow because we are telling the story.

Some participants are shy and do not wish to speak at all on stage. To these students I assign non-speaking parts and technical roles such as sound operator and stage manager. However, I always get everybody on stage at some point, even if it is just for the final group speech, because I want every group member to experience what it is like to be on a stage as part of an ensemble.

CASTING THE PLAY

Young people can be self-conscious and nervous with "formal" auditions, especially if they have little or no acting experience.

I conduct what I call an "informal" audition process. I hand out a questionnaire asking students if there is any particular role that they desire, whether they play a musical instrument. To get a feel for them as people, I also ask them to list one or two hobbies or interests. Occasionally this will inform my casting decisions. If someone can juggle, and the play has the part of a Fool, that skill may come in handy. Dancing or martial arts abilities can also be applied to roles.

For the auditions, I do not use the cut script. I have students stand and read from the Folger edition of the complete text in order to hear how they fare with the longer passages. I encourage them to breathe and carry their vocal energy all the way to the end of a long line of text. I also urge them to play with diction, projection, modulation, and dynamics, elements of speech that we have worked on in our vocal warm-ups and theater games.

I base my casting choices largely on reading ability, vocal strength, and enthusiasm for the project. If someone has requested a particular role, I try to honor that request. I explain that even with a small part, an actor can create a vivid character that adds a lot to the play. Wide variations in personality types can be utilized: if there are two students cast as Romeo, one brooding and one effusive, I try to put the more brooding Romeo in an early lovelorn scene, and place the effusive Romeo in the balcony scene. Occasionally one gets lucky, and the doubling of characters provides a way to match personality types with different aspects of a character's personality. But also be aware of the potential serendipity of non-traditional casting. For example, I have had one of the smallest students in the class play a powerful Othello. True power comes from within!

Generally, I have more females than males in a class, so women are more likely (and more willing) to play male characters than vice versa.

Rare is the high school boy who is brave enough to play a female character, which is unfortunate because it can reap hilarious results.

GET OUTSIDE HELP

Every time there is a fight scene in one of the plays I am directing, I call on my friend Michael Tolaydo, a professional actor and theater professor at St. Mary's College, who is an expert in all aspects of theater, including fight choreography. Not only does Michael stage the fight, but he does so in a way that furthers the action of the play, highlighting character's traits and bringing out the best in the student actors. Fight choreography must be done by an expert or somebody could get hurt. In the absence of such help, super slow motion fights are always a safe bet and can be quite effective, especially when accompanied by a soundtrack on the boom box.

During dress rehearsals I invite my friend Hilary Kacser. a Washington-area actor and dialect coach for two decades. Because I bring her in late in the rehearsal process, I have her direct her comments to me, which I then filter and relay to the cast. This avoids confusing the cast with a second set of directions. This caveat only applies to general directorial comments from outside visitors. Comments on specific artistic disciplines such as dance, music, and stage combat can come from the outside experts themselves.

If you work in a school, you might have helpful resources within your own building, such as a music or dance teacher who could contribute their expertise to a scene. If nobody is available in your school, try seeking out a member of the local professional theater. Many local performing artists will be glad to help, and the students are usually thrilled to have a visit from a professional performer.

LET STUDENTS BRING THEMSELVES INTO THE PLAY

The best ideas often come from the students themselves. If a young actor has a notion of how to play a scene, I will always give that idea a try. In a rehearsal of *Henry IV, Part 1,* one traveler jumped into the other's arms when they were robbed. It got a huge laugh. This was something that they did on instinct. We kept that bit for the performance, and it worked wonderfully.

As a director, you have to foster an environment in which that kind of spontaneity can occur. The students have to feel safe to experiment. In the same production of *Henry IV,* Falstaff and Hal invented a little fist bump "secret handshake" to use in the battle scene. The students were having fun and bringing parts of themselves into the play. Shakespeare himself would have approved. When possible I try to err on the side of fun because if the young actors are having fun, then they will commit themselves to the project. The beauty of the language, the story, the characters, and the pathos will follow.

There is a balance to be achieved here, however. In that same production of *Henry IV, Part 1,* the student who played Bardolph was having a great time with her character. She carried a leather wineskin around and offered it up to the other characters in the tavern. It was a prop with which she developed a comic relationship. At the end of our thirty-minute *Henry IV, Part 1,* I added a scene from *Henry IV, Part 2* as a coda: The new King Henry V (formerly Falstaff's drinking and carousing buddy Hal) rejects Falstaff, banishing him from within ten miles of the King. It is a sad and sobering moment, one of the most powerful in the play.

But at the performance, in the middle of the King's rejection speech (played by a female student, and her only speech), Bardolph offered her flask to King Henry and got a big laugh, thus not only upstaging the King but also undermining the seriousness and poignancy of the whole scene. She did not know any better; she was bringing herself to the character as I had been encouraging her to do. But it was inappropriate, and in subsequent seasons, if I foresaw something like that happening as an individual joyfully occupied a character, I attempted to prevent it. Some things we cannot predict. Now I make sure to issue a statement warning against changing any of the blocking on show day, and to watch out for upstaging one's peers.

FOUR FORMS OF ENGAGEMENT: VOCAL, EMOTIONAL, PHYSICAL, AND INTELLECTUAL

When directing a Shakespeare play with a group of students, I always start with the words themselves because the words have the power to engage the emotions, mind, and body. Also, I start with the words in action, as in the previously mentioned exercise, "Positive and Negative Salutations." Students become physically engaged; their bodies react to the images the words evoke. The words have the power to trigger a switch in both the teller and the listener, eliciting both an emotional and physical reaction. I have never heard a student utter the line "Fie! Fie! You counterfeit, you puppet you!" without seeing him change before my eyes. His spine stiffens, his eyes widen, and his fingers point menacingly.

Having used Shakespeare's words to engage the students emotionally and physically, one can then return to the text for a more reflective discussion of what the words mean to us personally. I always make sure to leave at least a few class periods open for discussion of the text, line by line, to ensure that students understand intellectually what they feel viscerally. The advantage to a performance-based teaching of Shakespeare is that by engaging students vocally, emotionally, and physically, it is then much easier to engage them intellectually because they are invested in the words, the characters, and the story. We always start on our feet, and later we sit and talk.

SIX ELEMENTS OF DRAMA: PLOT, CHARACTER, THEME, DICTION, MUSIC, AND SPECTACLE

Over two thousand years ago, Aristotle's *Poetics* outlined six elements of drama, in order of importance: Plot, Character, Theme, Diction, Music, and Spectacle. Because Shakespeare was foremost a playwright, it is helpful to take a brief look at these six elements as they relate to directing a Shakespeare play in the classroom.

PLOT (ACTION)

To Aristotle, plot was the most important element. One of the purposes of *The 30-Minute Shakespeare* is to provide a script that tells Shakespeare's stories, as opposed to concentrating on one scene. In a thirty-minute edit of a Shakespeare play, some plot elements are necessarily omitted. For the sake of a full understanding of the characters' relationships and motivations, it is helpful to make short plot summaries of each scene so that students are aware of their characters' arcs throughout the play. The scene descriptions in the Folger editions are sufficient to fill in the plot holes. Students can read the descriptions aloud during class time to ensure that the story is clear and that no plot elements are neglected. Additionally, there are one-page charts in the Folger editions of *Shakespeare Set Free,* indicating characters' relations graphically, with lines connecting families and factions to give students a visual representation of what can often be complex interrelationships, particularly in Shakespeare's history plays.

Young actors love action. That is why *The 30-Minute Shakespeare* includes dynamic blocking (stage direction) that allows students to tell the story in a physically dramatic fashion. Characters' movements on the stage are always motivated by the text itself.

CHARACTER

I consider myself a facilitator and a director more than an acting teacher. I want the students' understanding of their characters to spring from the text and the story. From there, I encourage them to consider how their character might talk, walk, stand, sit, eat, and drink. I also urge students to consider characters' motivations, objectives, and relationships, and I will ask pointed questions to that end during the rehearsal process. I try not to show the students how I would perform a scene, but if no ideas are forthcoming from anybody in the class, I will suggest a minimum of two possibilities for how the character might respond.

At times students may want more guidance and examples. Over thirteen years of directing plays in the classroom, I have wavered between wanting all the ideas to come from the students, and deciding that I need to be more of a "director," telling them what I would like to see them doing. It is a fine line, but in recent years I have decided that if I don't see enough dynamic action or characterization, I will step in and "direct" more. But I always make sure to leave room for students to bring themselves into the characters because their own ideas are invariably the best.

THEME (THOUGHTS, IDEAS)

In a typical English classroom, theme will be a big topic for discussion of a Shakespeare play. Using a performance-based method of teaching Shakespeare, an understanding of the play's themes develops from "mining the text" and exploring Shakespeare's words and his story. If the students understand what they are saying and how that relates to their characters and the overall story, the plays' themes will emerge clearly. We always return to the text itself. There are a number of elegant computer programs, such as www.wordle.net, that will count the number of recurring words in a passage and illustrate them graphically. For example, if the word "jealousy" comes up more than any other word in *Othello,* it will appear in a larger font. Seeing the words displayed by size in this way can offer up illuminating insights into the interaction between words in the text and the play's themes. Your computer-minded students might enjoy searching for such tidbits. There are more internet tools and websites in the Additional Resources section at the back of this book.

I cannot overstress the importance of acting out the play in understanding its themes. By embodying the roles of Othello and Iago and reciting their words, students do not simply comprehend the themes intellectually, but understand them kinesthetically, physically, and emotionally. They are essentially *living* the characters' jealousy, pride, and feelings about race. The themes of appearance vs.

reality, good vs. evil, honesty, misrepresentation, and self-knowledge (or lack thereof) become physically felt as well as intellectually understood. Performing Shakespeare delivers a richer understanding than that which comes from just reading the play. Students can now relate the characters' conflicts to their own struggles.

DICTION (LANGUAGE)

If I had to cite one thing I would like my actors to take from their experience of performing a play by William Shakespeare, it is an appreciation and understanding of the beauty of Shakespeare's language. The language is where it all begins and ends. Shakespeare's stories are dramatic, his characters are rich and complex, and his settings are exotic and fascinating, but it is through his language that these all achieve their richness. This leads me to spend more time on language than on any other element of the performance.

Starting with daily vocal warm-ups, many of them using parts of the script or other Shakespearean passages, I consistently emphasize the importance of the words. Young actors often lack experience in speaking clearly and projecting their voices outward, so in addition to comprehension, I emphasize projection, diction, breathing, pacing, dynamics, coloring of words, and vocal energy. *Theatre Games for Young Performers* contains many effective vocal exercises, as does the Folger's *Shakespeare Set Free* series. Consistent emphasis on all aspects of Shakespeare's language, especially on how to speak it effectively, is the most important element to any Shakespeare performance with a young cast.

MUSIC

A little music can go a long way in setting a mood for a thirty-minute Shakespeare play. I usually open the show with a short passage of music to set the tone. Thirty seconds of music played on a boom box operated by a student can provide a nice introduction to the play, create an atmosphere for the audience, and give the actors a sense of place and feeling.

iTunes is a good starting point for choosing your music. Typing in "Shakespeare" or "Hamlet" or "jealousy" (if you are going for a theme) will result in an excellent selection of aural performance enhancers at the very reasonable price of ninety-nine cents each (or free of charge, see Additional Resources section). Likewise, fight sounds, foreboding sounds, weather sounds (rain, thunder), trumpet sounds, etc. are all readily available online at affordable cost. I typically include three sound cues in a play, just enough to enhance but not overpower a production. The boom box operator sits on the far right or left of the stage, not backstage, so he can see the action. This also has the added benefit of having somebody out there with a script, capable of prompting in a pinch.

SPECTACLE

Aristotle considered spectacle the least important aspect of drama. Students tend to be surprised at this since we are used to being bombarded with production values on TV and video, often at the expense of substance. In my early days of putting on student productions, I would find myself hamstrung by my own ambitions in the realm of scenic design.

A simple bench or two chairs set on the stage are sufficient. The sense of "place" can be achieved through language and acting. Simple set dressing, a few key props, and some tasteful, emblematic costume pieces will go a long way toward providing all the "spectacle" you need.

In the stage directions to the plays in *The 30-Minute Shakespeare* series, I make frequent use of two large pillars stage left and right at the Folger Shakespeare Library's Elizabethan Theatre. I also have characters frequently entering and exiting from "stage rear." Your stage will have a different layout. Take a good look at the performing space you will be using and see if there are any elements that can be incorporated into your own stage directions. Is there a balcony? Can characters enter from the audience? (Make sure that they can get there from backstage, unless you want them waiting in the lobby until their entrance, which may be impractical.) If possible, make sure to rehearse in that space a few times to fix any technical issues and perhaps discover a few fun staging variations that will add pizzazz and dynamics to your own show.

The real spectacle is in the telling of the tale. Wooden swords are handy for characters that need them. Students should be warned at the outset that playing with swords outside of the scene is verboten. Letters, moneybags, and handkerchiefs should all have plentiful duplicates kept in a small prop box, as well as with a stage manager, because they tend to disappear in the hands of adolescents. After every rehearsal and performance, I recommend you personally sweep the rehearsal or performance area immediately for stray props. It is amazing what gets left behind.

Ultimately, the performances are about language and human drama, not set pieces, props, and special effects. Fake blood, glitter, glass, and liquids have no place on the stage; they are a recipe for disaster, or, at the very least, a big mess. On the other hand, the props that are employed can often be used effectively to convey character, as in Bardolph's aforementioned relationship with his wineskin.

PITFALLS AND SOLUTIONS

Putting on a play in a high school classroom is not easy. There are problems with enthusiasm, attitude, attention, and line memorization, to name a few. As anybody who has directed a play will tell you, it is always darkest before the dawn. My experience is that after one or two days of utter despair just before the play goes up, show day breaks and the play miraculously shines. To quote a recurring gag in one of my favorite movies, *Shakespeare in Love:* "It's a mystery."

ENTHUSIASM, FRUSTRATION, AND DISCIPLINE

Bring the enthusiasm yourself. Feed on the energy of the eager students, and others will pick up on that. Keep focused on the task at hand. Arrive prepared. Enthusiasm comes as you make headway. Ultimately, it helps to remind the students that a play is fun. I try to focus on the positive attributes of the students, rather than the ones that drive me crazy. This is easier said than done, but it is important. One season, I yelled at the group two days in a row. On day two of yelling, they tuned me out, and it took me a while to win them back. I learned my lesson; since then I've tried not to raise my voice out of anger or frustration. As I grow older and more mature, it is important for me to lead by example. It has been years since I yelled at a student group. If I am disappointed in their work or their behavior, I will express my disenchantment in words, speaking from the heart as somebody who cares about them and cares about our performance and our experience together. I find that fundamentally, young people want to please, to do well, and to be liked. If there is a serious discipline problem, I will hand it over to the regular classroom teacher, the administrator, or the parent.

LINE MEMORIZATION

Students may have a hard time memorizing lines. In these cases, see if you can pair them up with a "buddy" and existing friend who will run lines with them in person or over the phone after school. If students do not have such a "buddy," I volunteer to run lines with them myself. If serious line memorization problems arise that cannot be solved through work, then two students can switch parts if it is early enough in the rehearsal process. For doubled roles, the scene with fewer lines can go to the actor who is having memorization problems. Additionally, a few passages or lines can be cut. Again, it is important to address these issues early. Later cuts become more problematic as other actors have already memorized their cues. I have had to do late cuts about twice in thirteen years. While they have gotten us out of jams, it is best to assess early whether a student will have line memorization problems, and deal with the problem sooner rather than later.

In production, always keep several copies of the script backstage, as well as cheat sheets indicating cues, entrances, and scene changes. Make a prop list, indicating props for each scene, as well as props that are the responsibility of individual actors. Direct the Stage Manager and an Assistant Stage Manager to keep track of these items, and on show days, personally double-check if you can.

In thirteen years of preparing an inner-city public high school English class for a public performance on a field trip to the Folger Secondary School Shakespeare Festival, my groups and I have been beset by illness, emotional turmoil, discipline problems, stage fright, adolescent angst, midlife crises (not theirs), and all manner of other emergencies, including acts of God and nature. Despite the difficulties and challenges inherent in putting on a Shakespeare play with a group of young people, one amazing fact stands out in my experience. Here is how many times a student has been absent for show day: Zero. Somehow, everybody has always made it to the show, and the show has gone on. How can this be? It's a mystery.

✳ PERFORMANCE NOTES: *THE MERCHANT OF VENICE*

I directed this production of *The Merchant of Venice* in 2013 with a group of high school seniors. Although the play is technically a "comedy," it is also one of Shakespeare's cruelest, depicting the harsh treatment of Shylock as well as an attitude of prejudice toward the Jewish people

Discuss with your students what experiences they may have had with prejudice. Also, ask them to look at the individual characters to explore what good and bad qualities they exhibit personally. Through examining our own experiences with intolerance, and by looking at discrimination through the eyes of Shakespeare's characters, we can better portray the complex individuals and relationships in this riveting drama.

I used a Chorus extensively in this production: in all three "courting" scenes as an entourage to the Princes and Bassanio, as well as in the courtroom scene as a jury or gallery. There are several advantages to choral work. First, it strengthens the group dynamic. Students who would otherwise have minor roles are onstage for longer, allowing for a greater level of participation. This contributes greatly to the overall feel of the performance as an ensemble production.

In addition, the Chorus reinforces the mood: When the action is funny, the Chorus makes it funnier! In Scene 6, all six Chorus members bump into Bassanio and each other, a comic moment that would have been far less effective with only one collision. Likewise, when the mood is harsher, the Chorus makes it downright brutal. When all the actors onstage shout, "Jew!" and point to Shylock, the impact is greater than if only one character had done so.

The Chorus provides visual and sound effects, verbal commentary, and emotional reactions to the action on the stage, which not only helps clarify the story but also adds to its power.

SCENE 1 (ACT II, SCENE II/ACT I, SCENE I)

The play opens with a speech from the clown character of Lancelet, who does not appear in the rest of this cutting. While Lancelet's words and demeanor set a lighthearted tone for the play, the phrase "the Jew . . . is a kind of devil" paints a harsh picture of the prevailing attitude of Christians toward Jews, with the remark tossed off casually as a light aside. Thus, the first words spoken in the play prepare us for laughter while setting the stage for darker themes.

The young woman playing Lancelet also plays Solarino directly following this introductory passage, which is why the stage directions read, *"Winks, replacing his hat with SOLARINO'S hat."* In our production, this hat exchange did not take place onstage; the actress changed her hat offstage and returned wearing a different hat as Solarino. Sometimes, ideas that look good on paper—such as the winking and changing hats onstage to indicate that one is going to return as a different character—don't read as well when actually performed.

What did work was the shift in vocal and physical mannerisms that the student playing Lancelet employed. As Lancelet, she was physically jumpy, almost falling from a standing to a sitting, cross-legged position after the line, "'Budge not,' says my conscience." To illustrate the internal battle between "the fiend" and Lancelet's conscience, the actor's eyes shifted from right to left and back, and on the line, "I will run, fiend. I will run," she leapt up and ran off the stage.

When she returned onstage as Solarino a few seconds later, wearing a different hat and vest, the actress chose to have her character speak and move more slowly and deliberately. Her facial expressions as Solarino were more somber and thoughtful than those of her Lancelet. Whenever a student actor is playing more than one character in a play, it is very helpful to depict each character with distinct physical traits and vocal styles, which clarifies the story for the audience.

Antonio's opening lines paint a verbal picture for the audience: "In sooth I know not why I am so sad." The actress playing Antonio had a lovely, wistful way of delivering the lines and enjoying their alliterative poetry. By contrast, Solanio's first line is, "Then let us say you are sad, because you are not merry." As always with Shakespeare, we discover who a character is by the specific words he says. If we choose which words to color and emphasize, the audience receives a richer portrait of the personage.

Bassanio's speech about Portia offers another opportunity for coloring of words as well as the power of a pause. The actor playing Bassanio gave a pause, or "beat," before saying the word "Portia." It is during this silent moment before Bassanio utters her name that he looks out over the audience with a faraway smile on his face. When he utters her name, "Portia," we have had a chance to glimpse on Bassanio's face what the word means to him. It is only by allowing themselves beats like this that actors can exploit the full potential of the emotional power of a person's name.

Other adjectives in Bassanio's speeches in this scene can be emphasized to further illustrate Portia's light in Bassanio's eyes. When he says the words "sunny," "golden," and "fair Portia," his tongue trips lightly over the words as his eyes twinkle in reflection of their imagery. I encourage young actors to take their time to coax these evocative images out of Shakespeare's words using their own vocal and physical interpretations.

SCENE 2 (ACT I, SCENE II)

The Narrator announces the terms of Portia's marriage, i.e., the suitor must choose the correct casket. She then wrinkles her forehead as if she is considering this arrangement and adds as a coda, "I wouldn't like that either." The audience laughs, once again because she gives it a beat. By making the facial expression before adding the extra line, the actor shares her thought process with the audience, which in turn gives them the incentive to laugh when the line emerges. When actors do not rush their lines, the drama and comedy have time to reach their full fruition.

There are some lovely pieces of stage business in this scene between Portia and Nerissa that illustrate that their relationship has more than one level. As the scene begins, Nerissa stands behind a seated Portia, combing Portia's hair as Portia looks at herself in a handheld mirror. When the conversation turns to a specific suitor, Bassanio, Nerissa moves next to Portia, and they speak while looking directly at each other and smiling. This indicates to the audience that although Nerissa is Portia's servant, she is also her friend and confidante.

At the mention of Bassanio, Portia leaps up excitedly from her chair and then, catching herself, sits back down and affects a studied casualness on "as I think he was called." Her delivery gets a laugh while simultaneously suggesting that although Portia is excitable, she is interested in presenting an image of being in control. At the end of the scene, Portia and Nerissa exit together, giggling, on equal footing. The staging of this short scene illustrates the difference in status between the two characters, as well as their underlying friendship.

SCENE 3 (ACT I, SCENE III)

Shylock holds a newspaper in his hand at the top of the scene. When he discusses with Bassanio the status of Antonio's ships, he points to the newspaper as if he has been reading this news. Props provide information about characters: Shylock, a merchant, keeps up with local business ventures.

Also, by reading the newspaper rather than look directly at Bassanio initially, Shylock puts himself in a position of power. By not looking Bassanio in the eye, Shylock paints a portrait of a man who does not necessarily observe social niceties, a point that subsequently affects the way Bassanio and Antonio regard him. Acting is reacting. If Shylock stood up smiling and shook Bassanio's hand, it would be a different story. Small staging choices go a long way toward setting up a conflict.

Shylock's "I hate him for he is a Christian" speech can be directed at the audience, and I encourage the actors to direct certain lines to individual audience members. This direct address pulls the audience in and helps make the story personal. By mining the text, students can find specific reasons why Shylock and Antonio, or by extrapolation, Jews and Christians, hate each other in this play.

The subject is one that is painful and touchy to examine, but in the context of drama and history, the issue of prejudice can be explored in a way that is equally healthy and revelatory. Both Shylock and Antonio have sympathetic and unkind qualities. By showing more than one side to their characters, actors paint a nuanced dramatic picture that allows us to see what motivates people to behave in objectionable ways. When we experience Shylock as a living, breathing human with noble qualities as well as tragic flaws, Shakespeare's words and stories have greater emotional depth and a deeper personal impact.

The actor playing Bassanio adds an effective beat to the end of the scene as he takes a moment to look worriedly at the horizon—over the audience's head—as if a storm is brewing.

SCENE 4 (ACT II, SCENE I/ACT II, SCENE VII)

There is almost nothing better than a good laugh. Our goal with the entrance of the Prince of Morocco was to elicit laughter from the audience, so we had the Prince and his entourage of six Chorus members enter dancing, loose and funky.

The Prince played a sprightly drumbeat on the hand drum, and the six chorus members danced behind him with flailing arms and happy feet, as if riding invisible horses, in what appeared to be the "Gangnam style" dance move that was popular that year. This piece of choreography worked; the audience laughed heartily, and the tone was set for a very funny scene.

This was the first of three consecutive scenes that used a comic Chorus to accompany each suitor. The Chorus members echoed some of the suitors' physical moves and recited or chanted aloud the note inside each casket, each recitation accompanied by rhythmic, simple movement. To make these Chorus bits work requires commitment from each Chorus member as well as a sense of fun. Fortunately, fun is contagious, so typically one or two Chorus members would bring the energy up by physically committing to the silliness. Manifestations of this commitment included fully extended limbs, animated facial expressions, and vertical leaps!

Simultaneous actions by both Morocco and the Chorus impart tightness to the visual theatrics. When Morocco draws the "curtains," he makes a clean gesture with both hands from the center of his body, which is echoed by the Chorus. Likewise, when he raises his hands up on "Some god direct my judgment," the Chorus makes the same gesture simultaneously. This use of the Chorus keeps more students engaged in the performance and rehearsals, significantly enhances the ensemble feel of the play, and provides a nod back to classical theater by using a technique made popular by the Greek chorus.

After Morocco chooses the wrong casket, he and his entourage dance out in unison despondently, heads down. Portia's final line is, "Let all of his complexion choose me so." This statement suggests that Portia has a prejudice toward dark-colored individuals, which can further student discussion about the role of prejudice in *The Merchant of Venice*. The scene between Portia and Morocco is funny and lighthearted, but some troubling sentiments boil below the surface.

SCENE 5 (ACT II, SCENE IX)

I am always amazed at how a simple gesture can change a theatrical moment for the better. The Narrator in this scene speaks the line, "Next up is the Prince of Arragon. Will he fare any better? Place your bets." This is the kind of line that could evoke a laugh but could just as easily fall flat. The student playing the Narrator chose to remove his hat from his head when saying, "Place your bets," holding the hat out toward the audience as if to collect money. He paused a second before doing so, which added an element of surprise and got a laugh. At every moment in a play, actors can make small choices, either through gesture, inflection, timing, or facial expression, to change the tone and even the meaning of a scene.

A young woman wearing a fake beard and mustache, which she twirled with verve, played the Prince of Arragon in our production. We chose to put fake mustaches on the Chorus members in her entourage as well, which gave them a silly and unified look. As in the previous scene, when the Prince takes the note out of the box, he turns toward the Chorus and shows it to them, who all again pretend to put a monocle on one eye so they can read it. When he is rejected, Arragon defiantly throws his head back, straightens his spine, and proudly dances out to a drumbeat, stopping to turn toward Portia and deliver a final dismissive wave, which the Chorus echoes. Repetition enhances comedy.

SCENE 6 (ACT III, SCENE II)

In the two previous scenes, Portia's suitors have been princes, so it made sense that they would have entourages. Bassanio is simply a citizen and thus would likely arrive unaccompanied to woo Portia. However, as in the previous two scenes, a drumbeat accompanies the Chorus, dancing behind Bassanio as he enters.

Bassanio is annoyed by this unrequested accompaniment, so he stops dead in his tracks and turns around to glare at the first Chorus member, who comes to a screeching halt. This causes the remaining Chorus members to bump into each other one by one and then sheepishly return to their position in a line upstage.

The audience responds with a big laugh. There is a rule of three in comedy, and since we had two setups to this moment with two prior Choruses, the disruption of the expectation coupled with the bumbling Chorus' multi-person pileup makes for a classic comedy moment.

The Chorus has a song in this scene, which they chant rhythmically, using gestures to illustrate certain words. When Bassanio moves to kiss Portia, all Chorus members lean in for a good look, and when the kiss takes place, the Chorus in unison coos, "Aww." In this production of *The Merchant of Venice*, the Chorus' ensemble work deservedly won an award at the Folger Secondary School Shakespeare Festival.

We had to work hard to achieve the unity of word and gesture that we were seeking. When one Chorus member is off, the whole group suffers. This is why we rehearse until we get it right. I consider this ensemble work to be one of the greater rewards of putting on a play with students. So much of their schoolwork is done at the individual level; it is gratifying to watch them experience the satisfaction of a successful group effort.

SCENE 7 (ACT IV, SCENE 1)

The courtroom scene opens with the familiar dance drumbeat to usher in the Chorus, who dances in, only to have the Duke stand up and yell, "Silence!" prompting them to stop dead in their tracks, unsmiling. This sets the tone for a scene that is definitively noncomedic. Antonio sits on the stool with his arms tied. When Shylock defends his insistence on a pound of Antonio's flesh, and asks, "Are you answered?" the Chorus, as one, sternly replies, "No!"

In Portia's speech explaining to Shylock his punishment if he sheds a drop of Christian blood, every time Portia says the word "Jew," the Chorus repeats it, first in a whisper, then louder, pointing fingers, and finally yelling the word at Shylock. The effect of this group speech and gesture is chilling. The Chorus, which before was dancing and silly, is now vindictive and cruel.

Just as comedy is funnier under a backdrop of sadness, so is tragedy more poignant when it has been preceded by laughter. *The Merchant of Venice* balances these comic and cruel elements masterfully as the Chorus points to Shylock and brings him to his knees as they yell, "Down!" In drama, a character will change as events unfold, and the young actor playing Shylock did an excellent job of depicting Shylock's transformation from a proud and haughty merchant to a beaten, pleading man.

SCENE 8 (ACT V, SCENE I)

The Merchant of Venice is classified as a comedy, and so it has a happy ending. However, as the Narrator at the top of this scene points out, "Everybody ends up happy. Except Shylock. Which is kind of a big 'except.'" The interchange between Lorenzo and Jessica establishes a mood of forgiveness and reconciliation. Their mock argument plays out best when both characters look back at each other simultaneously, having placed themselves back to back in feigned insult.

Despite the lighthearted reconciliations that end the play, I made a directorial choice to end this cutting with a choral rendition of Shylock's "I am a Jew" speech, which he commences solo and is then joined by the entire cast. Upon watching the video of this production, with Shylock standing in the center of the stage surrounded by the cast, asking the questions, "If you prick us, do we not bleed? And if you wrong us, shall we not revenge?" I could not help but shed a tear.

Shakespeare's *The Merchant of Venice* is a powerful play with themes of bigotry and intolerance that apply to any era. By experiencing this timeless story together, our ensemble and the audience gained insight into what motivates human cruelty, with enough levity provided to make us laugh.

Live theater is magical. It is the most dynamic form of entertainment available to us. *The Merchant of Venice* is a powerful drama, and we are fortunate to be able to keep giving the story life, particularly with young performers who can give the play the vitality it deserves.

✳ *THE MERCHANT OF VENICE:* SET AND PROP LIST

SET PIECES:

Table
Two stools

PROPS:

SCENE 1:

Three mugs
Wineskin or wine bottle

SCENE 2:

Hairbrush for Nerissa
Hand mirror for Portia

SCENE 3:

Newspaper for Shylock

SCENE 4:

Hand drum
Three boxes: one painted gold, one painted silver, and one
    painted lead color or made of metal
Key for Portia to give to Morocco
Skull containing rolled-up scroll (placed inside gold casket)
Small fool's head and rolled-up scroll (placed inside silver
    casket for Scene 5)
Photo of Portia and rolled-up scroll (placed inside lead

casket for Scene 6)

SCENE 6:

Large bag of coins for Chorus to give to Portia
Five small bags of coins for Chorus to give to Portia

SCENE 7:

Large scroll for Shylock's bond
Bag of coins for Bassanio to offer Shylock
Knife for Shylock

SCENE 8:

Piece of paper (deed of gift) for Nerissa to give to Lorenzo

The Merchant of Venice

By William Shakespeare

Performed by Banneker Academic High School
Mr. Feeser's Twelfth Grade AP English Class

Folger Secondary School Shakespeare Festival | Tuesday, March 26th, 2013
Instructor: Mr. Charles Feeser | Guest Director: Mr. Nick Newlin

CAST:

Scene 1 (Act I, Scene 1): Venice, A street
Lucentio (Suitor to Bianca): Jason McKenzie
Lancelet: Parris Washington
Narrator: Nelly Quintanilla
Antonio: Andranae Nelson
Solarino: Parris Washington
Solanio: Ashley Jones
Bassanio: Jovanne Santouse

Scene 2 (Act 2, Scene 2): Belmont, A room in Portia's house
Narrator: Ashley Jones
Portia: Jennifer Betancourt
Nerissa: Asia McCray-James

Scene 3: (Act 1, Scene 3): Venice, A public place
Narrator: Lauren Robinson
Shylock: Maximilian Younginer!
Bassanio: Jovanne Santouse
Antonio: Andranae Nelson

Scene 4: (Act 2, Scene 1 and Act 2, Scene 7): Belmont, A room in Portia's house
Narrator: Olive Nwosu
Morocco: Frankey Grayton II
Chorus: Parris Washington, Nelly Quintanilla, Ashley Jones, Olive Nwosu, Tariq Broadnax, Lauren Robinson!
Portia: Jennifer Betancourt
Nerissa: Asia McCray-James

Scene 5: (Act 2, Scene 9) Belmont: A room in Portia's house
Narrator: Tariq Broadnax
Nerissa: Asia McCray-James
Portia: Tameisha Thorpe
Arragon: Sylverline Atufu
Chorus: Parris Washington, Nelly Quintanilla, Ashley Jones, Olive Nwosu, Tariq Broadnax, Lauren Robinson

Scene 6: (Act 3, Scene 2) Belmont, A room in Portia's house
Narrator: Parris Washington
Portia: Tameisha Thorpe
Nerissa: Asia McCray-James
Bassanio: Jovanne Santouse
Gratiano: Tariq Broadnax
Chorus: Parris Washington, Nelly Quintanilla, Ashley Jones, Olive Nwosu, Tariq Broadnax, Lauren Robinson

Scene 7 (Act 4, Scene 1) Venice, A court of justice
Narrator: Nelly Quintanilla
Duke: Yasmeen Wicks
Antonio: Andranae Nelson
Shylock: Maximilian Younginer
Bassanio: Jovanne Santouse
Nerissa (disguised as lawyer's clerk): Asia McCray-James
Portia (disguised as Balthazar, a doctor of law): Asia Hart
Chorus: Parris Washington, Nelly Quintanilla, Ashley Jones, Olive Nwosu, Tariq Broadnax, Lauren Robinson

Scene 8 (Act 5, Scene 1): Belmont, Avenue to Portia's house
Narrator: Parris Washington
Lorenzo: Nelly Quintanilla
Jessica: Olive Nwosu
Portia: Asia Hart
Nerissa: Asia McCray-James
Bassanio: Jovanne Santouse
Antonio: Andranae Nelson

Drums: Frankey Grayton II

> *"The pound of flesh, which I demand of him,*
> *Is dearly bought; 'tis mine and I will have it."*
> —*Shylock*

ADDITIONAL RESOURCES

SHAKESPEARE

Shakespeare Set Free: Teaching Romeo and Juliet, Macbeth and a Midsummer Night's Dream
Peggy O'Brien, Ed., Teaching Shakespeare Institute
Washington Square Press
New York, 1993

Shakespeare Set Free: Teaching Hamlet and Henry IV, Part 1
Peggy O'Brien, Ed., Teaching Shakespeare Institute
Washington Square Press
New York, 1994

Shakespeare Set Free: Teaching Twelfth Night and Othello
Peggy O'Brien, Ed., Teaching Shakespeare Institute
Washington Square Press
New York, 1995

The *Shakespeare Set Free* series is an invaluable resource with lesson plans, activites, handouts, and excellent suggestions for rehearsing and performing Shakespeare plays in a classroom setting.

ShakesFear and How to Cure It!
Ralph Alan Cohen
Prestwick House, Inc.
Delaware, 2006

The Friendly Shakespeare: A Thoroughly Painless Guide to the Best of the Bard
Norrie Epstein
Penguin Books
New York, 1994

Brush Up Your Shakespeare!
Michael Macrone
Cader Books
New York, 1990

Shakespeare's Insults: Educating Your Wit
Wayne F. Hill and Cynthia J. Ottchen
Three Rivers Press
New York, 1991

Practical Approaches to Teaching Shakespeare
Peter Reynolds
Oxford University Press
New York, 1991

Scenes From Shakespeare:
A Workbook for Actors
Robin J. Holt
McFarland and Co.
London, 1988

THEATER AND PERFORMANCE

Impro: Improvisation and the Theatre
Keith Johnstone
Routledge Books
London, 1982

A Dictionary of Theatre Anthropology:
The Secret Art of the Performer
Eugenio Barba and Nicola Savarese
Routledge
London, 1991

THEATER GAMES

Theatre Games for Young Performers
Maria C. Novelly
Meriwether Publishing
Colorado, 1990

Improvisation for the Theater
Viola Spolin
Northwestern University Press
Illinois, 1983

Theater Games for Rehearsal:
A Director's Handbook
Viola Spolin
Northwestern University Press
Illinois, 1985

101 Theatre Games for Drama
Teachers, Classroom Teachers
& Directors
Mila Johansen
Players Press Inc.
California, 1994

PLAY DIRECTING

Theater and the Adolescent Actor:
Building a Successful School Program
Camille L. Poisson
Archon Books
Connecticut, 1994

Directing for the Theatre
W. David Sievers
Wm. C. Brown, Co.
Iowa, 1965

The Director's Vision: Play Direction
from Analysis to Production
Louis E. Catron
Mayfield Publishing Co.
California, 1989

INTERNET RESOURCES

http://www.folger.edu
The Folger Shakespeare Library's
website has lesson plans, primary
sources, study guides, images,
workshops, programs for teachers
and students, and much more. The
definitive Shakespeare website for
educators, historians and all lovers
of the Bard.

http://www.shakespeare.mit.edu.
The Complete Works of
William Shakespeare.
All complete scripts for *The
30-Minute Shakespeare* series were
originally downloaded from this site
before editing. Links to other internet
resources.

http://www.LoMonico.com/
Shakespeare-and-Media.htm
http://shakespeare-and-media
.wikispaces.com
Michael LoMonico is Senior
Consultant on National Education
for the Folger Shakespeare Library.
His *Seminar Shakespeare 2.0* offers a
wealth of information on how to use
exciting new approaches and online
resources for teaching Shakespeare.

http://www.freesound.org.
A collaborative database of sounds
and sound effects.

http://www.wordle.net.
A program for creating "word clouds"
from the text that you provide. The
clouds give greater prominence to
words that appear more frequently in
the source text.

http://www.opensourceshakespeare
.org.
This site has good searching capacity.

http://shakespeare.palomar.edu/
default.htm
Excellent links and searches

http://shakespeare.com/
Write like Shakespeare,
Poetry Machine, tag cloud

http://www.shakespeare-online.com/

http://www.bardweb.net/

http://www.rhymezone.com/
shakespeare/
Good searchable word and phrase
finder.
Or by lines:
http://www.rhymezone.com/
shakespeare/toplines/

http://shakespeare.mcgill.ca/
Shakespeare and Performance
research team

http://www.enotes.com/william-
shakespeare

Needless to say, the internet goes on and on with valuable Shakespeare resources.
The ones listed here are excellent starting points and will set you on your way in the
great adventure that is Shakespeare.

NICK NEWLIN has performed a comedy and variety act for international audiences for thirty-two years. Since 1996, he has conducted an annual play directing residency affiliated with the Folger Shakespeare Library in Washington, D.C. Newlin received a BA with Honors from Harvard University in 1982 and an MA in Theater with an emphasis in Play Directing from the University of Maryland in 1996.

THE 30-MINUTE SHAKESPEARE

AS YOU LIKE IT
978-1-935550-06-8

THE COMEDY OF ERRORS
978-1-935550-08-2

HAMLET
978-1-935550-24-2

HENRY IV, PART 1
978-1-935550-11-2

HENRY V
978-1-935550-38-9

JULIUS CAESAR
978-1-935550-29-7

KING LEAR
978-1-935550-09-9

LOVE'S LABOR'S LOST
978-1-935550-07-5

MACBETH
978-1-935550-02-0

A MIDSUMMER NIGHT'S DREAM
978-1-935550-00-6

THE MERCHANT OF VENICE
978-1-935550-32-7

THE MERRY WIVES OF WINDSOR
978-1-935550-05-1

MUCH ADO ABOUT NOTHING
978-1-935550-03-7

OTHELLO
978-1-935550-10-5

RICHARD III
978-1-935550-39-6

ROMEO AND JULIET
978-1-935550-01-3

THE TAMING OF THE SHREW
978-1-935550-33-4

THE TEMPEST
978-1-935550-28-0

TWELFTH NIGHT
978-1-935550-04-4

THE TWO GENTLEMEN OF VERONA
978-1-935550-25-9

THE 30-MINUTE SHAKESPEARE ANTHOLOGY
978-1-935550-33-4

All plays $9.95, available in print and eBook editions in bookstores everywhere

"A truly fun, emotional, and sometimes magical first experience . . . guided by a sagacious, knowledgeable, and intuitive educator." —Library Journal

PHOTOCOPYING AND PERFORMANCE RIGHTS

There is no royalty for performing any series of *The 30-Minute Shakespeare* in a classroom or on a stage. The publisher hereby grants unlimited photocopy permission for one series of performances to all acting groups that have purchased the play. If a group stages a performance, please post a comment and/or photo to our Facebook page; we'd love to hear about it!